let's travel in

HAWAII

Edited by Darlene Geis

A TRAVEL PRESS BOOK

PICTURE ACKNOWLEDGMENTS

The full-color pictures in this book were taken in Hawaii by the following photographers and artists, whose collaboration is gratefully acknowledged. For the pictures Josef Muench (1, 2, 3, 4, 5, 6, 8, 11, 13, 14, 15, 16, 17, 19, 20, 21, 22, 23, 24, 25, 26, 27, 29, 31 and 32); Wolfe Worldwide Films, California (10, 12 and 30); Ewing Krainin, from Monkmeyer (7, 9 and 28); Fritz Henle, from Monkmeyer (18). For the black-and-white photographs we wish to thank the Hawaii Visitors Bureau; Fritz Henle, from Photo Researchers, Inc.; Bernd Lohse, from Rapho-Guillumette; the Bettmann Archieve; and the American Museum of Natural History. The map was made by Enrico Arno.

New edition published 1965 by CHILDRENS PRESS, INC., Chicago.
Published simultaneously in Canada. Lithographed in the U.S.A.
Library of Congress Catalog Card Number: 65-15977

CONTENTS

PACIFIC
KAUAI
Hanalei Bay
HANALEI VALLEY
WAIMEA CANYON
MT. WAIALEALE
Wailua R.
Waimea
24
25
26
27
28
29
30
31
NIIHAU
OAHU
1-12
Honolulu
MOLOKAI
LANAI
OAHU
Laie
WAIANAE RANGE
KOOLAU RANGE
Pearl Harbor
Honolulu Harbor
Diamond Head
1
2
3
4
5
6
7
8
9
10
11
12

Locales of thirty-two full-page pictures

HAWAII,

PARADISE IN THE PACIFIC...

IN THE broad blue reaches of the Pacific Ocean lies a strand of islands like small green gems strung on a wavering line. From northwest to southeast they stretch for about 1,500 miles, following the course of an ancient cleft in the ocean floor thousands of feet below. When the ocean bottom split millions of years ago, volcanic rock surged out of the long crack, forming a mountain ridge in the dark underwater depths. Submarine volcanoes continued their hidden activity until finally the mountain range was built up to a height of 18,000 feet and the Hawaiian Islands burst through the surface of the sparkling expanse of the Pacific.

The northwestern islands were probably the first to be thrust up into the sunlight. They are the oldest, and volcanic activity long ago ceased on them. But at the southeastern end of the chain the mountains still smoke and rumble, and thick streams of molten lava flow sluggishly to the sea, where they harden and extend the shore line of the still-growing island of Hawaii.

In the warm Pacific waters, coral reefs have formed on some of the lava rock, and there is a sprinkle of small coral islets, mostly uninhabited, among the larger volcanic islands. But mainly, when we speak of the Hawaiian Islands, we mean the eight principal green gems that stretch for about 400 miles, and lie almost in the center of the ocean at the crossroads of the Pacific. North America, South America, Australia and Asia are the four continents circling this vast body of water, with Hawaii at its heart. "The loveliest fleet of islands that lies anchored in any ocean," is the way Mark Twain described these lush isles of greenery. Now the Fiftieth State in the Union, with a total area of 6,407 square miles, Hawaii adds a new and shining star to the flag of the United States.

THE FIRST HAWAIIANS

The beautiful bits of land moored in mid-Pacific were unknown and uninhabited until about 500 A.D. Then Polynesians from the island of Samoa or Tahiti, venturing out on the vast empty ocean, finally beached

Four continents circle the broad Pacific, with Hawaii at its heart.

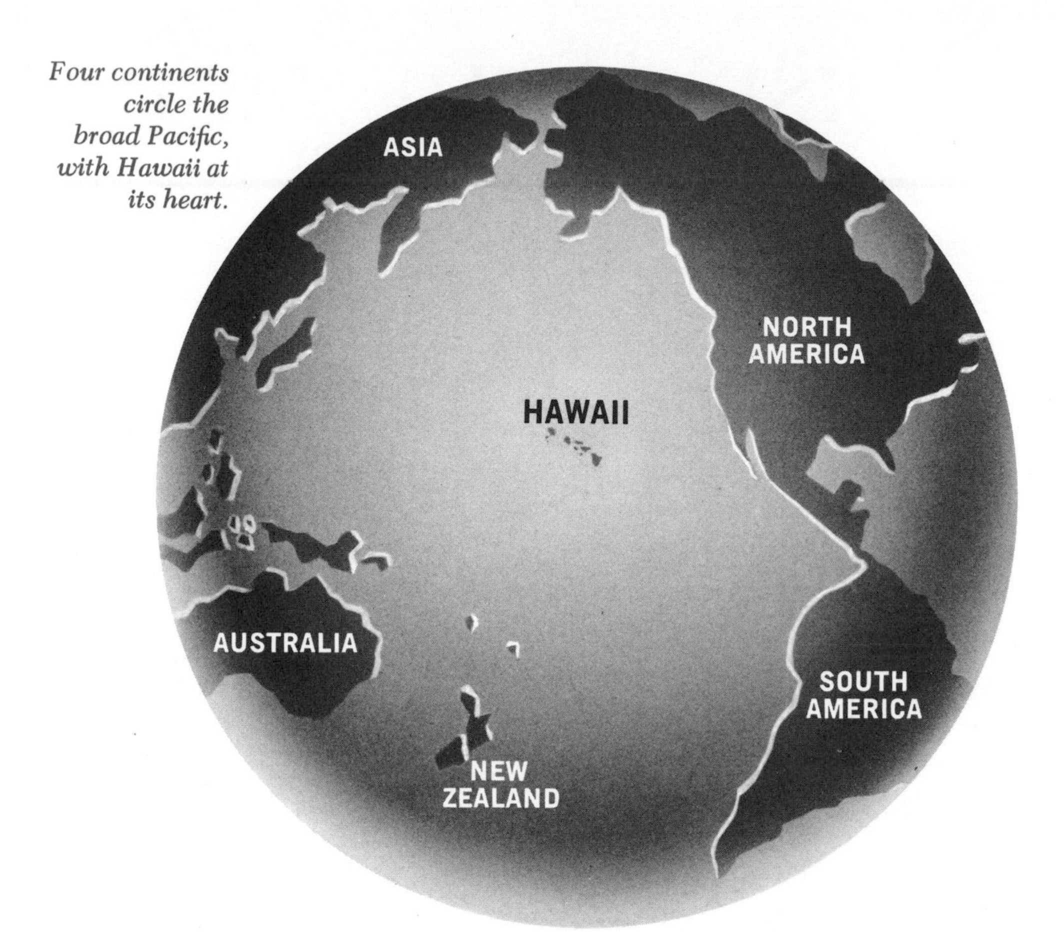

their canoes on a strange shore, and they called the place Hawaii. These early Hawaiians had a religion based on gods that demanded human sacrifices, and their kings and priests were all-powerful. The men were superb athletes, remarkable sailors and navigators, and great fishermen. They were also fierce warriors, and the tropical paradise that was their home was not the untroubled and peaceful land that we might imagine.

A complex system of taboos made life difficult and oppressive for the ordinary people. Their daily concern was to avoid committing any of the trivial acts that were punishable by death. A man and woman could not eat together, for example, and certain choice foods were taboo for women. If a person's shadow fell on any taboo object, he was immediately killed. Nevertheless, in spite of the harshness of their laws, these were gentle people—courteous, hospitable and kindly—and there was an innocence and beauty in their lives. They loved singing and dancing and story-telling, and much of their history and wisdom was handed down by their performing artists. Their craftsmen were especially skilled in the delicate and painstaking featherwork that was used in fashioning helmets, capes, *leis* (LAYS) and robes for the Hawaiian nobility. The few examples of this art remaining today are literally beyond price.

Into this world of handsome and intelligent bronze-skinned people the white man came one day, bringing inevitable changes. Many were good—some were not. Now it is those traces of a vanished and lovely native culture that the visitor to Hawaii cherishes most. The flower *leis,* the hula dance and the *luau* (*loo*-AU), or feast, are the popularized echoes of Hawaii's past.

CAPTAIN COOK'S DISCOVERY

The first white man to sight the miraculous islands jutting out of the Pacific was Captain James Cook, the bold British voyager. Cook was looking for the Northwest Passage when he came upon Hawaii by lucky accident in 1778. Landing on the island of Kauai (KAU-*eye*), he was greeted by hundreds of natives who threw themselves at his feet, believing him to be one of their gods. Cook and his crew (one of whom was Lieutenant Bligh, later famous as the captain of the Bounty) were given a royal Hawaiian welcome. They traded iron nails for food and native handicrafts, including several magnificent yellow-and-red-feathered royal capes, which are now bright treasures in the British Museum.

In honor of his patron, the Earl of Sandwich, Captain Cook called the islands the Sandwich Islands. (This unromantic name was later abandoned.) In 1779 Cook returned to the islands once again, this time landing on Hawaii. Again he was treated like a god, but he and his men were needlessly brutal in their dealings with the natives. A fight broke out, and Cook was killed on the beach while attempting to get back to his ship.

The hidden paradise had been discovered, and soon other ships from other lands began to make the Sandwich Islands a port of call. Whaling vessels and trading ships put in for supplies. They introduced firearms, rum and disease to a people who had not known them before. On the credit side they also brought seeds and livestock. But the pure and primitive Polynesian chapter of Hawaiian history had come to a close.

KAMEHAMEHA, KING OF THE ISLANDS

Soon after the arrival of the white man, one of the native chiefs, aided by firearms and the shrewd advice of two marooned British sailors, set about the conquest of all the Hawaiian Islands. Kamehameha (*kah*-MAY-*hah*-MAY-*hah*) I, in a series of brilliant campaigns, managed to bring all the islands under his domination, with the exception of Kauai. He ruled justly and wisely until 1819, and gave Hawaii the strength and unity of a single country, and a dynasty which would continue his leadership through the years of increasing foreign influence.

When the great king died, the drastic powers of the old pagan religion died with him. Two of his queens brazenly broke the taboos—one ate coconut, forbidden to women, and the other sat down to feast in public with her son, the new king. The people watched in horror, but there was no divine retribution. Instead the high priest leapt up and set fire to his temple with the cry, "The gods die!" Hawaii was ready for the coming of the missionaries.

THE GREAT CONVERSION

In 1820 the first little group of missionary families landed on the island of Hawaii after a six months' voyage from Boston. The blue lagoons and whispering palm trees, the golden-bronze bodies and pagan delight in pleasure were a challenge to these strict and dedicated New Englanders. They lost no time in clothing the muscular Hawaiian men in long pants and the graceful ladies in shapeless Mother Hubbards. Then they set about the practical business of teaching the word of God to heathens without a written language. Out of their efforts came a systematized Hawaiian alphabet, and textbooks, Bibles and newspapers were soon being printed in the Hawaiian language. Not long after, Christianity became the national religion of the islands.

Other American missionaries followed the first group, and their work laid the foundation for the future close relationship between Hawaii and the United States. The natives, with their quick intelligence, were apt and eager pupils, and the New Englanders were zealous teachers.

Today Hawaii has one of the finest educational systems in the United States, and its classrooms are filled with children of many races and backgrounds, who are learning together. In a little over a century it has changed from a remote and exotic Polynesian kingdom to an enlightened community of a mixture of peoples, only five hours by jet from mainland United States.

OAHU, THE ALOHA ISLAND

The chief educational, cultural and business center of all the islands is Oahu (*oh-AH-hoo*), third largest island of the group. Its name means "gathering place," and its harbor and airport are among the busiest in the world. Honolulu (HONE-*oh-loo-loo*), the capital of Hawaii, stretches along the Pacific coast, with blue water in front of it and green mountains rising behind it. Arriving here, the visitor is greeted with fragrant flower *leis* and the traditional Hawaiian word of friendly welcome—"*aloha*" (*ah*-LOW-*hah*). At once he catches the overtones of old Hawaii amid the bustle of this modern city. The dazzling stretch of palm-fringed white sand known as Waikiki (*wye-kih*-KEE) Beach is a miniature South Seas Riviera. This section of Honolulu, with its row of luxurious hotels, is most particularly the gathering place of tourists.

The United States Pacific Fleet is based in the great land-locked port of Pearl Harbor, adjoining Honolulu. Here the infamous attack of December 7, 1941, has left as a memorial the rusted hulks of the battleships *Utah* and *Arizona,* where over a thousand American dead are still entombed. The partly sunken wreck of the *Arizona,* with her ghostly crew aboard, still flies the American flag. The colors are raised and lowered each morning and evening by a naval honor guard.

HAWAII, THE BIG ISLAND

An hour's flight from Honolulu is the largest, youngest and most easterly island of the chain, which gave the entire group its name. Hawaii is twice as large as all the other islands put together. Two of its mountains tower over 13,000 feet—Mauna Kea (MAW-*nah* KEH-*ah*), or "White Mountain," and Mauna Loa (LOW-*ah*), or "Long Mountain." Mauna Loa and a smaller volcano, Kilauea (*key-lau*-AY-*ah*), put on spectacular eruptions every few years, and visitors fly over just to watch the impressive sight. The ancient Hawaiian fire-goddess Pele (PAY-*leh*), whose name means "volcano," supposedly lives on Hawaii. According to ancient superstition, it is she who tends the fiery furnaces and hurls the flaming red lava out of the boiling depths. The people living on the seven other islands must be delighted that Pele settled on Hawaii.

In contrast to the awesome majesty of its volcanoes, Hawaii also has the peaceful tropical beauty of an ideal South Sea island. Orchids are shipped from Hawaii to the mainland, and this island has become the largest center of orchid culture in the United States.

MAUI, THE VALLEY ISLAND

Maui (MAU-*ee*) is the second largest island of the chain, and it was at one time, in the nineteenth century, the capital of the kingdom of Hawaii. Probably Maui and its three neighboring islands were once joined together, but now they are separated by narrow channels. Of these three islands, Lanai (LAH-*nigh*) is owned by a pineapple company; Kahoolawe (*kah-hoo*-LAH-*vay*) is an uninhabited island used for target practice; and Molokai (*moh-loh*-KY) is seldom visited, though it, too, has its share of tropical beauty.

On the island of Maui, visitors see one of the great natural marvels of the world. The immense dormant crater of Haleakala (*hah-leh-ah-kah*-LAH), whose floor is 25 square miles in area, rests like a giant bowl beneath the tropical sky. Ancient Hawaiians believed that at one time the sun was lassoed and held captive here, and looking at this crater brimming with sunshine, we can understand the origin of that legend.

KAUAI, THE GARDEN ISLAND

Kauai, a forty-five-minute flight to the west of Oahu, is the firstborn of the Hawaiian Islands. Because it is older, it has thicker soil and is more verdant and lush than any of the others. This is the island that King Kamehameha was never able to subdue. But when he died, one of his widows united it with the other islands by marrying both the king and the prince of Kauai simultaneously, in what must have been an unusual triple-ring ceremony.

Hawaii's first sugar plantation was on this fertile island, whose name means "Abundance of Good." Now the sugar industry is the largest in the islands, producing about $145,000,000 worth of raw cane sugar a year. Pineapple is the second largest industry in Hawaii, and there are pineapple plantations on Kauai, as well as on the other islands. The third big business of the Fiftieth State is tourism, and Kauai holds its own in tourist attractions, too. Its Waimea (*wy*-MAY-*ah*) Canyon, cut out of brightly colored volcanic rock, is one of the most stupendous sights in all Hawaii.

Each of the islands has a palmy tropical loveliness that runs in the family, but each has some distinctive beauty mark not found on any of the others. The visitor who never ventures beyond the island of Oahu will certainly see something of Hawaii, but he will have missed many of its greatest delights.

Now let us join the thousands of travelers who yearly cross the miles of blue Pacific to refresh and renew themselves on these magic islands.

Every visitor is given a kiss and a lei aboard the incoming boat.

let's travel in

PARADISE REGAINED: WELCOME TO HAWAII

ONLY a few hours by jet and we are in another world! When we alight from the plane, the balmy air carries the scent of thousands of flowers and the promise of lazy days and nights in these warm and pleasant islands. The welcome of the islands is in the smile of this proudly beautiful Hawaiian woman.

The people who inhabit these islands have a special beauty that combines a look of ancient wisdom with present vitality. They are completely different from the people found on the mainland of the United States. Hawaii's heritage came from half a world away. Hawaiian girls have long been noted for their beauty and the lovely face in this picture shows us why. The first people who made these islands their home were pure Polynesian. Now there are only about 10,000 pure-blooded Hawaiians, compared with the 300,000 who inhabited the islands when Captain Cook landed there in 1778.

These were always a handsome and noble people. Today the islanders include strains from most of the countries of the East—Japanese, Korean, Chinese, Filipino—as well as from several European nationalities. Nowhere has the blending of many peoples achieved more beautiful results. The racial amity of Hawaii is as much a part of it as the combers racing past Diamond Head or the rare flowers deep in its forests.

The traditional warmth and friendliness of the Hawaiians remain a great part of their charm today. Their heartfelt spirit of welcome enfolds the traveler as tangibly as the gentle caress of the Hawaiian air. And you sense that this is not merely a well-staged performance which visitors have come to expect, but a genuine expression of pleasure from these islanders.

LEI VENDOR: LANGUAGE OF FLOWERS

VISITORS arriving in Hawaii are greeted with the grace and hospitality typical of its legendary past. They are serenaded with island music thrummed on ukuleles, and are festooned with garlands of fresh flowers. In this picture we see one of the unofficial greeters near the airport. There is a row of these little grass shacks, each with its owner's name on it—"Susan's," "Dottie's," "Emma's" and, in this picture, "Martha's." The sweet-smelling flower *leis* are a colorful symbol of Hawaiian welcome, and the women who sell and make them might have stepped right out of the islands' past.

Martha is wearing the long shapeless dress, made of bright printed cotton and called a *muumuu (moo-moo)*, that stems from the Mother Hubbards introduced by modest missionary wives. In her hands is a *lei* of red carnations. Long ago, *leis* were made of feathers and were worn only by royalty, as a badge of authority and high station. As the intricate featherwork became more rare because the island birds were dying out, flowers, which were equally brilliant, were substituted.

Friends usually give arriving and departing passengers these *leis.* But they can be bought for a very small price, and as you can see, the variety of colors and blossoms is endless. It takes from thirty-five to seventy-five flowers to make a *lei,* so these delicate works of art are inexpensive by mainland standards. Orchids, jasmine, pale yellow ginger, gardenias and the bright red lehua (*lay*-HOO-*ah*), State flower of Hawaii, are just some of the island flowers used. Their brilliance and fragrance speak eloquently the Hawaiian word "*aloha,*" which means "welcome," but can also mean "farewell" or "love."

MARTHA'S

ALOHA
10

ALOHA TOWER: HONOLULU LANDMARK

BEFORE the age of air travel, it was this tower that every visitor saw first when his ship steamed into Honolulu harbor. Rising slim and white near the dock where the *Lurline,* queen of Hawaiian passenger ships, has her berth, this famous landmark is remembered fondly by thousands of tourists to Hawaii. The large clock on each of its four sides is topped by that friendly word of welcome, "*aloha,*" as if to indicate that the hours it measures will be warm and pleasant ones.

Nowadays, even if you arrive in Honolulu by plane, you will probably visit the Aloha Tower early in your stay. It is literally one of the high points of the city and offers a superb view and a chance to orient yourself in Honolulu. An elevator takes tourists to the tenth-floor observation gallery and from this vantage point city and harbor spread out below like a living map. When you look out over Honolulu, you will understand the unusual system of directions used here. "North," "south," "east" and "west" are terms you will not hear. Instead, *mauka* (MAU-*kah*), which means "toward the mountains," is north; *makai* (*mah*-KY), or "toward the sea," is south; *ewa* (EV-*vah*), the name of the sugar plantation and mill to the west, is west; *Waikiki,* the name of the beach to the east, is east. If we stand on the observation gallery of the Aloha Tower and look north toward the mountains or south toward the sea, directions in Honolulu style are dramatized as mere compass points never could be.

Pearl Harbor, near Honolulu, is the base for the United States Pacific fleet.

HARBOR SCENE: VACATION SHIP

THIS great ship moored to her dock in Honolulu harbor is one of the luxury passenger liners running on a regular schedule between California and Hawaii. The trip west takes four and a half days, and its climax is the gala arrival in Honolulu. Boats have always been tremendously important to the islanders because nearly everything in Hawaii must be imported. They are a tie with the outside world, which lies miles and miles beyond the boundless blue horizon. So on boat day the docks are jammed with islanders who have come down to welcome their floating link with the mainland.

When a liner comes to port, the Royal Hawaiian Band is on the dock with a group of Hawaiian singers. Gay throngs add to the noise and revelry, and flower *leis* make bright daubs of color in the crowd. The *Lurline* usually docks in the morning, after having been met off shore by a launch filled with jubilant greeters, including some grass-skirted hula dancers. So by the time the beautiful white ship gets to its dock the passengers are well in the swing of things. While the *Lurline* is being tied up, the water around the ship is alive with the flashing brown bodies of native boys, who dive for coins thrown from the decks. They are as much a part of any tropical harbor scene as the scavenging sea gulls that wheel and dart over the waters of northern harbors.

Once the passengers and boat-day crowds depart, the *Lurline* is readied for her return voyage. Again there will be music and crowds and *leis* and hula dancers. But this time there will be undertones of sadness as the band plays "*Aloha Oe*," the nostalgic "Farewell to You," written by one of Hawaii's queens. As the ship moves slowly away from the dock, the passengers lining her rails observe one final tradition of the islands. They throw their *leis* overboard. If the garland floats toward shore, that is a sign that its owner will return one day.

M

WAIKIKI BEACH: ETERNAL SUMMERTIME

AT LAST we are on the beach at Waikiki, celebrated in song and travel poster and in the enthusiastic reports of people who have been there. This narrow strip of clean white sand stretches for a little over a mile, and reaches almost to the point of land where Diamond Head juts boldly out into the Pacific. Slanting palm trees grow along the beach, and behind them tower the fabulous hotels with picture windows and tiers of balconies—a far cry from the thatched huts that used to stand here.

As we look at Waikiki Beach, it is impossible to tell whether it is June or January. In Honolulu the average summer temperature is 78 degrees; the average winter temperature is 72 degrees. And even the rain is considerate. Generally the lee shores of all the islands have a very light rainfall. The trade winds, blowing from the northeast across the Pacific, strike the windward coasts and spill their cargo of water on those shores and on the mountaintops. Waikiki and Honolulu, on the lee side of Oahu, have very little rain, and what the islanders do have they choose to call "liquid sunshine."

The ocean, too, is mild, and the bathers at Waikiki can count on water always a few degrees warmer than the balmy air. Much as those seen in this picture are enjoying themselves on the noonday beach, it is even more romantic and delightful to swim by moonlight or torchlight. The mild night air and the gentle ocean make this a perfect diversion for a tropical evening.

No view of Waikiki would be complete without the sharp prow of Diamond Head in the background. Although it looks as solid as the Rock of Gibraltar, when you see it from the air you realize that it is the crater of a dead volcano. The massive profile of Diamond Head is really just the rim of the hollow crater, cold now and with patches of green growing in the rocky bowl.

SURFBOARD RIDER: THE SPORT OF KINGS

THERE is something regal about the assured yet careless stance of this young man riding the surfboard. Seeing him speed toward shore, balancing on a slim board that skims the crest of a thirty-mile-per-hour breaker, we can believe that in olden times this was the royal game. In those days there was an exacting ritual which governed the sport. For it was not only a test of skill and athletic prowess; it was the chosen sport of kings and queens, and they undertook it only with their gods' help. They also used an especially buoyant wood for the royal surfboards. The best beaches were reserved for them, and at Waikiki there are still sections of beach called Queen's Surf and King's Surf in memory of those times.

But surfboarding in early days was popular chiefly because it was an exciting gambling game. Commoners and royalty alike wagered recklessly on the outcome of surfing contests. A man could lose everything—his house, his wife, even his own freedom—if he backed the wrong rider. The thrill of danger was as great for those watching on the beach as it was for the performers who dared the crashing surf a mile from shore. The missionaries put a quick stop to the hectic game, and it was not revived until early in this century. Then an American renewed interest in surfboarding purely as a sport and game of skill.

Waikiki is the best and most famous beach for surfing. A coral reef runs parallel to the shore about a third of a mile out, and it causes the ocean to break into long and powerful rollers that surge straight in to the beach. The glistening brown athlete we see here is doing exactly what his royal ancestors did. First he paddles out to where the breakers are forming. Then he heads for shore, still lying on his board and paddling until one of the great waves catches him at its crest. With his board zooming along on top of the wave, the rider rises to his feet and shoots toward the beach like a jet-propelled merman.

KA MOI

ALOHA WEEK: FESTIVAL OF PAST GLORIES

ALTHOUGH much of Hawaiian pageantry that harks back to the old days of the great kings is put on for tourists, it still has a certain haunting reality. When we see the celebrations today we cannot help being stirred by them.

We see here the opening ceremonies of Aloha Week, an eight-day festival that takes place every October. It begins with the arrival of the "king" in that most traditional Hawaiian water vehicle, the double canoe. On a platform bridging two canoes, the tall king stands with his warrior chiefs. The old Hawaiian rulers were gigantic people, taller and more powerfully built than their subjects, and a king or queen sometimes weighed from 300 to 500 pounds. His Majesty wears the royal cloak of golden feathers, and a feather helmet that bears a startling resemblance to the crested headpiece of ancient Greeks. His courtiers carry kahilis (KAH-*hee-lehs*), tall feather-topped standards that are the emblem of kingship.

Later the "queen" will arrive in a similar canoe, attended by warriors and followed by a fleet of outriggers manned by lesser chiefs. When the boats land on the beach, the pageant will proceed to a nearby park. For the rest of the week there will be numerous events, including a daring and skillful outrigger race, a hula festival and re-enactments of ancient Hawaiian ceremonies.

Aloha Week attracts an audience of about 100,000 spectators, and nearly 6,000 Hawaiians take part in the show. Yet when we watch the spectacle against the backdrop of Diamond Head and the blue Pacific, it seems authentic. The ancestors of these people sailed in just such a canoe over this very ocean, guided by the stars to these green islands. It is hard to believe that when Aloha Week is over, the majestic "king" in this picture will abdicate and become once again the modest citizen of a modern state.

KING KAMEHAMEHA: ISLAND MONARCH

IN downtown Honolulu the statue of Hawaii's greatest king has a commanding place in front of the Judiciary Building. The handsome bronze monument is probably one of the most photographed tourist attractions in the islands, and it is unusual to see it this way, minus an entourage of camera-happy visitors. On holidays the statue is hung with dozens of fresh flower *leis* in tribute to a colorful king.

The Hawaiian Legislature voted to spend $10,000 for a monument to Kamehameha. The statue was cast by master artisans in Italy and then was sent by ship to Honolulu. The ship sank, and the statue went down with it. But since it was insured, another casting was made, and in 1883 this noble bronze was placed where we see it now. Years later the sunken ship was salvaged, and the statue of the Hawaiian king was found to be none the worse for its immersion. It was bought by the government, and now stands high and dry on a courthouse lawn on Hawaii Island, the birthplace of Kamehameha.

The only throne room in the United States is part of Iolani Palace, where Hawaiian monarchs reigned.

We get some feeling of the greatness of the man himself from his sculptured likeness. Strength, dignity and courage have been cast in bronze. Kamehameha was called the Napoleon of the Pacific, but looking up at this statue one begins to think that it was the Little Corporal who was flattered.

KAMEHAMEHA I

GOODS
KRESS
KRESS
DRESS SHOP

HONOLULU: METROPOLIS OF THE PACIFIC

KING Kamehameha probably wouldn't recognize this busy modern city as the capital of his islands. As a matter of fact, when we stand on this street corner and look around, there is nothing particularly "Hawaiian" about it, even to our eyes. But a more careful second look tells the story. The women in their long *muumuus* and the men in gaudy *aloha* shirts help to give Honolulu its local color. And on a street corner such as this, the passing parade illustrates the broad gamut of racial strains that is so distinctive of modern Hawaii. We encounter Chinese, Japanese, Filipino, Puerto Rican, Portuguese, Polynesian and Caucasian faces in the crowd. And there are many mixtures and combinations that would be difficult to identify. President Eisenhower called Hawaii "a unique example of a community [that is] a successful laboratory in human brotherhood."

Visitors to Hawaii tend to think of it as a land of beaches and palm trees and languorous living. But they are surprised to learn that more than half of all the people in Hawaii are concentrated in Honolulu—a city of nearly 300,000 people. Beautiful tropical Hawaii is predominantly urban.

Before World War II, Hawaiian business was largely in the hands of a small group of island families. Since the war and the tremendous influx of Armed Forces personnel, many mainland businesses have opened branches in Honolulu.

Native atmosphere is never very far away —we find it even here, on Waikiki's main street.

MORMON TEMPLE: MISSIONARY MONUMENT

NO, we are not in India, though this Mormon temple has been called the Taj Mahal of Hawaii. We have only traveled straight across the island of Oahu, and are at Laie (*lah*-EE-*eh*) on the windward shore. Finding a building like this one on the outskirts of a small native village is one of the many delightful surprises that Hawaii has to offer. The Mormons have a large following on the Islands, where they have built many small churches. They have a tabernacle in Honolulu, but this temple at Laie is exceptional in that it is the only Mormon temple outside North America. It was built in 1919, and cost $300,000. The rigid and rather formal landscaping and the severe elegance of the white building seem out of place, perhaps, in this country of casual lagoons and wind-tossed palm trees. But its very incongruity makes it even more striking.

The Mormons came to Hawaii some thirty years after the Boston missionaries had laid the groundwork for Christianity here. They founded a colony on little Lanai Island, and it thrived. Then they moved to Oahu where their sect has continued to grow. To this day you can see a number of young missionaries going on foot through the Islands, working to win converts to the Mormon faith. Here at Laie, visitors may follow the paths that lead up the landscaped terraces to the temple, but first they must attend a lecture about the Latter-Day Saints in a small auditorium nearby.

Once a month the natives of Laie, most of whom are Mormons, stage a community fishing party and *luau* for visitors from Honolulu and other parts of the island. After the feast there is dancing—the hula and other Polynesian dances. This brilliant day-long party is given to raise funds for the Mormon Church, and it is one of the most popular events on the island.

TRADITIONAL LUAU: OLD-STYLE BARBECUE

LUAUS used to be community feasts that were held in every Hawaiian village on special occasions. They were as gala as any national festival anywhere. The gay and festive spirit is still part of a luau, but now it is frequently dressed up with all the trimmings of a tourist attraction. The big hotels arrange a luau once a week, and in many of the villages throughout Hawaii they are staged to raise money. The price of a ticket depends on the size of the luau.

In this scene we are watching the main event—the native preparation of a pig—which is a day-long chore. The whole pig is stuffed with hot rocks. It is then carefully lowered into a pit filled with red-hot rocks and covered over with leaves. There it stays in its underground oven, called an imu (EE-*moo*), and when the roasted pig is finally lifted out and ready for the feast, its meat falls away in tender shreds. Like most of the foods at a *luau,* the pig was meant to be eaten without utensils.

Luau means taro leaf, and originally the foods at these native feasts were wrapped in taro leaves when they were served. Pieces of beef and chicken and fish are also roasted in the imu, and the feast is one of great variety and color. Some of the native concoctions are unpleasantly strange to tourists' palates. *Lomilomi* (LOW-*mee*-LOW-*mee*), for example, is a raw salmon that has been vigorously massaged under water, then shredded and mixed with onion, tomato and a special red salt. Not recommended for those who like their fish cooked, with the original flavor preserved.

HULA DANCERS: RHYTHM OF THE ISLANDS

THE hula is the dance for which Hawaii is famous, although what we frequently see is a popularized version of it. In early times the hula was an important part of old Hawaiian culture. Since the people had no written language, their history and folklore were handed down by means of a kind of Polynesian opera. Singers, dancers and musicians re-enacted the well-loved stories of the race, and their every gesture meant something. When these dancing girls arch their fingertips, they are telling us about a rainbow; when their hands meet in a point, they are describing a star.

Correct hula is performed as these girls are doing it, with the feet flat on the ground, knees bent and the body swaying from side to side as the weight shifts. Meanwhile, the hands and arms tell the story. But the missionaries found the dances shocking. They tried to mend matters by dressing the girls in middy blouses and full skirts, but there were still distractions from the story line. Finally hula was banned altogether, and a valuable native art form was nearly lost.

Then the jolly monarch King Kalakaua (*kal*-UH-*kau-ah*) revived the native dance during his reign, towards the end of the last century. The original pre-missionary dancers had worn brief tapa-cloth skirts and flower *leis*. But King Kalakaua introduced a new note. He had sent one of his ships to take over all the South Sea isles. It failed in its grandiose mission, but the captain brought back a gift from the chief of Samoa. It was a grass skirt. Today the island dancers are more likely to wear skirts made of leaves instead of grass, in a return to the old authentic Polynesian hula.

ISLE OF HAWAII: DRAMATIC SHORE LINE

THIS is how the islands must have looked before a living soul ever set foot on them. One of the wonderful things about Hawaii is that you can fly from a big modern city like Honolulu and in a little over an hour be in a place of utterly unspoiled beauty, such as we see here. We are on the eastern shore of Hawaii, the Big Island, and this is the black sand beach of Kalapana (*kah-lah-*PAH*-nah*). The surf creaming along the edges of dark sand and the grove of slim palm trees rustling against the sky create a vision of tranquillity all too rare in the world today.

Yet this is far from being a tranquil island. A few miles from this idyllic beach is the crater of Kilauea, whose fire pit still smolders and erupts. Volcanic rock and boulders fallen from its slopes have been shattered by the sea and ground into the black sands of Kalapana. Further inland, Mauna Loa occasionally dazzles the world with a pyrotechnic display. For this is the home island of the ancient Hawaiian fire-goddess Pele. Natives here still think they see her sometimes, a wandering witch with long strands of fiery hair, who appears in order to warn people of the next volcanic eruption.

Life is simple in this primitive paradise—a beachfront lot, three boats, but no running water.

GARDENS OF HILO: POLYNESIAN EDEN

ALL nature seems to erupt in riotous color on the island of Hawaii. Hilo (HEE-*low*), where we are now, is famous for its flowers, and particularly for orchids. It is called "the orchid capital," and fifty million of the festive blossoms are flown to the United States each year. But while orchids might be the aristocrats of the garden, there are hundreds of other tropical flowers that bloom here, adding vivid accents to the greenery. There are about nine hundred species of flowering plants on these small islands, so the range of colors, shapes and scents is enormous. No wonder Hawaiians deck themselves so lavishly with flowers—the living jewels of the Islands.

Looking at this picture of richly blooming Hilo it is difficult for us to remember that the city has suffered frightful destruction from tidal waves. In 1946 a giant tidal wave washed into the harbor, moving at a speed of 450 miles an hour. Eight more great waves followed, and they demolished a large part of the city and took a dreadful toll of human lives. In 1960 disaster struck again, but the city has blossomed once more, as hardy and vigorous as the plants that burgeon here with so little coaxing.

Behind Hilo, the snow-capped crater of Mauna Kea gleams against the clear blue sky. You can leave this tropical garden and go skiing less than thirty-five miles away. And on the other side of the volcano, the vast Parker Ranch stretches over 300,000 acres. Only one ranch in the United States—the King Ranch in Texas—is larger. The Hawaiian cowboys, called *paniolas* (*pahn-ee-*OH*-lahs*), learned their trade from Mexican ranch hands brought over for that purpose. But they have added one distinctive and typical touch to their costumes. They sometimes wear hatbands of flowers on their ten-gallon hats.

PARK AT HILO: JAPANESE FANTASY

ON THE shores of Hilo Bay, where the land juts out into the Pacific, there is a lovely park in honor of Hawaii's last queen. Liliuokalani (*lih-lee-oh-kah-*LAH-*neh*) Park has been landscaped by Japanese gardeners, and except for the palm trees screening the distant shore, it is like a bit of Japan transplanted to Hawaii. Actually there are more Japanese living on the islands than any other single racial group—190,000 of them. Buddhist temples, teahouses and the Cherry Blossom Festival in April add a dash of the Orient to the Hawaiian mixture.

In the nineteenth century, when sugar was first planted on a large scale, labor had to be imported to keep up with the growing demands of the plantations. Thousands of Chinese and Japanese workers were brought to the islands to toil patiently in the cane fields. Some returned to their own countries with their savings and some went to the mainland in search of better opportunities, but many stayed on in Hawaii and raised families. Before World War II, the loyalty of the Japanese-Americans was suspect, but a thorough investigation of their activities in Hawaii by the F.B.I. during the war and the brilliant war record of many of the island-born Nisei dispelled any doubts as to the quality of their citizenship. It was these young Hawaiian men of Japanese parentage who were in the "Purple Heart Battalion" that saw action at Salerno, Anzio and Cassino. One of the men who served in the valiant Japanese-American battalion in World War II is Daniel K. Inouye. He has been Hawaii's member of the House of Representatives. And Hiram L. Fong, a Chinese-American businessman, has been one of Hawaii's Senators. The status of the Oriental citizens in the United States is certain to have a profound effect upon her relationship with the Asiatic peoples of the world.

NATIVE FISHERMAN: TRICKY NET-CASTING

ON THE western side of Hawaii Island, the past reaches back to the earliest days of Hawaiian history. Here, near Kona (KOO-*nah*), old Hawaii lives again. We see it in this picture of a native fisherman, who is using a technique perfected by his ancestors. The circle of net is edged with weights, and the fisherman stands on the shore, or on a rock in shallow water. He searches the clear shallows with a sharp eye. Then when he sees his fish he lets fly with the net. This primitive form of lassoing a fish with a throw-net still brings results. At night you can see Hawaiians wade out knee-deep in the water, and armed with spears and torches—and their own keen eyes—snag a respectable catch.

But the tourist who comes to the historic Kona Coast is frequently lured there by its exceptional deep-sea fishing. He can charter a boat with friends for very little. The boat is equipped with a fish-god to be rubbed for good luck. The fish-god brought record-breaking luck to one visitor who hauled in a 796-pound fish. Marlin, sailfish, barracuda, dolphin, bonito and tuna disport themselves in the deep off-shore waters. But our man in this picture is after smaller fish, though he must pit himself against them with equal skill and cunning.

Commercial fishing is an important island industry, though it's more fun to catch fish yourself.

GOLDEN PAPAYA: FRUIT OF THE TROPICS

OF ALL of the larger islands in the group, Hawaii is the only one where pineapple is not grown commercially. There are sugar plantations, cattle ranches and fields of orchids, and on the west coast near Kona several small coffee plantations are perched in the hills. A number of other tropical fruits grow here, too. In this picture a native girl is standing beneath the giant tropical papaya. This fruit tree comes originally from Central America and, like nearly everything else that grows on these islands, was brought here by settlers. The bare volcanic mountain peaks that rose above the water might have been dependent for their greenery at first upon birds carrying seeds. The tides washed up growing plants or seeds that later took root on the rocky shores.

The first Polynesian "Vikings of the Sunrise," who rowed here in huge double canoes, brought some foods, and later white settlers introduced avocados, mangoes, pineapples, passion fruit, coffee, litchis, dates and papayas. This girl may well be proud of the size of the fruit she is showing us. Papaya grows from three to twenty inches in length, and this is certainly a king-size variety. It is a popular breakfast fruit on the Islands, and its golden-pink flesh is slightly sweet, with a rather musky taste. In different climates the taste varies, and in California, for example, while papayas grow beautifully, the flavor is not comparable. The milky juice of the fruit contains papain—something like pepsin and an excellent digestive that the natives use in various remedies.

All of the tropical fruits seem to have captured the exotic flavor of the Islands. And visitors who learn to eat mangoes or papayas here find that when they eat them again at home, memories of this tropical land come flooding back with each taste.

FERN FOREST: PRIMEVAL WORLD

A LARGE tract of land that includes the eastern slopes of Mauna Loa and Kilauea Crater is now part of Hawaii National Park. The other part of the park is on the neighboring island of Maui, and its main attraction is another remarkable volcanic crater which we are going to visit later.

One of the most awesomely beautiful parts of the park on Hawaii Island is the tree fern forest. Further up, the volcanic crater rises harsh and bare, but at the foot of the mountain, where the heavy rains encourage growth, the luxuriant ferns make a dense mysterious jungle. In this picture we are in one of several similar forests in the Islands. We can only think longingly of the life led by the early Polynesians in spots of primitive beauty such as this. When we look at this scene, however, we ought to take into account the malevolent god brooding over the quiet forest, and we must also realize that the rainfall hereabout is uncomfortably heavy. So much for Eden.

Visitors have looked covetously at many of the articles of Hawaiian life and have managed to acquire them without the discomforts of really going native. The brilliantly flowered cotton fabrics are now made up into dresses and shirts that would be as acceptable in anyone's back yard as they are in this primeval forest. Even the sarong has been adopted—à la Hollywood. The objects made from woven strips of pandanus leaves have found favor with mainlanders, too, and visitors buy mats, bags, purses and hats, sophisticated in style but primitive in material. The grotesque Polynesian idols carved from soft fern wood are among the strangest souvenirs of the Islands. Some old idols used to adorn the pagan temples before the missionaries came. Now the original forms are being carved again from the trunks of giant tree ferns —in small sizes suitable for packing. However "touristy" the souvenirs are, when they are seen in their rightful setting these articles gain in dignity and beauty.

HAWAIIAN HATMAKER: SOUVENIRS FOR TOURISTS

THIS placid barefoot man, wrapped in a few yards of printed cotton and wearing a garland of flowers around his neck, symbolizes a hundred-million-dollar-a-year Hawaiian industry. Tourism has become Big Business in the islands; in an average year more than 200,000 visitors are given a warm *"aloha."* Hotels, restaurants, shops and inter-island travel facilities have boomed to keep up with the ever-increasing crowds. In the native villages along the coast of Hawaii Island, the old handicrafts have been revived in a manner certain to appeal to the tourist, his camera—and his checkbook.

Against a background of old-style grass shacks and in time to popular versions of island songs, native girls string *leis* of tropical flowers. Native men weave strips of coco palm leaves into broad-brimmed hats that will be worn jauntily on the beach at Waikiki—but not by natives. People are recognized as tourists by the native clothes they wear.

Hawaii has always had the problem of balancing her imports with her exports. The islanders point out that only the climate and the scenery are native. Everything and everyone else had to be brought to the islands. There is little—besides sugar and pineapple—that Hawaii has had to offer in exchange for the necessities which she must import. But now with tourists flocking to her pleasant shores, her economy is sounder—thanks in part to men like our palm-leaf weaver and their indispensable souvenirs.

Even the littlest tourists enjoy the beauties of Hawaii.

ISLE OF MAUI: COCONUT CLIMBER

ROUGHLY halfway between Hawaii and Oahu, the island of Maui is the second largest of the group. Here on one of its beaches a Hawaiian boy performs the age-old gymnastic feat of the tropics, scaling a coconut tree. Coconut palms did not originally grow in the Islands. The early Hawaiians brought them from their tropical homeland to the south, with taro, breadfruit, yams, bananas and arrowroot, and all of these plants thrived, adding to the living green that eventually clothed the bare volcanic rock. To the old Hawaiians, coconut was a food for men only, and women stole a bit of this delicacy only on pain of death. As we look at this picture, the taboo makes sense. Imagine a man shinnying up the tall, rough trunk of a palm tree and knocking down a coconut. And then imagine him sliding down to the ground with scraped knees, only to find that his mate has walked off with the coconut and is happily sharing it with "the girls." One such man must have muttered, "There ought to be a law," and the taboo was born.

Hawaiian mythology is filled with colorful personalities and delightful stories. One of the most famous demigods was Maui, for whom this island is named. He was responsible for the existence of all the Hawaiian islands. One day Maui went fishing, and his line caught on something very heavy. He pulled up a vast mass of land from the floor of the Pacific, but his line snapped under the weight, and the land broke into eight islands. A look at our map will show you that it *might* have happened that way.

When the first white men sailed to the islands and dropped anchor, the natives rowed out to greet them joyously.

LAHAINA: OLD WHALERS' PORT

LAHAINA (*lah*-HIGH-*nah*), on the western shore of Maui, is a romantic port. Kamehameha's son made it the capital of his dusky monarchy, and so it remained for about twenty-five years. But in 1845, when the court moved to Honolulu, the whalers took over. The great roadstead, offering protected anchorage for whalers' ships, was an ideal port in which to spend the winter. The whalers were a rough and rowdy bunch, and had little respect for law and order. The Boston missionaries who had worked hard in Lahaina, were horrified by the moral decline of the town.

Finally the government stepped in and cleaned up the town. They built a good-sized prison and filled it with all those who had freely cooperated in breaking the local laws. One of the best roads on the island was supposedly built by these island prisoners. However it was the New England missionaries who brought religion to the islands that left a more lasting memorial than their salty compatriots. The school for teachers which they built with the help of their students in 1831 is still in existence. It was there that the first newspaper to be published west of the Mississippi went to press.

In this picture we see the Pioneer Hotel, a waterfront inn that dates from about 1900. Recently it was restored by a group of Hawaiian businessmen. In memory of the by-gone whaling days in Lahaina, the hotel has a sign in front of its bar that says, "Old Whalers' Grog Shoppe." It also flies the Hawaiian flag beneath Old Glory. Hawaii borrowed the Union Jack from Great Britain, and added eight stripes (for her eight main islands).

SUGAR PLANTATION: SWEET SUCCESS

MAUI, the Valley Island, has the largest sugar planting in the islands. This crop, which shaped Hawaii's destiny, is the foundation upon which her economy rests. No one knows how sugar cane first came here. Captain Cook reported that the natives used it for hedges around their huts, so it was here before the white man came. The climate is ideal for it. Sugar needs a great deal of water—one pound of sugar uses nearly two tons of water while it is growing. And Hawaii is blessed with an abundance of water. On Maui there are 370 inches of rain each year on the western mountains.

As we can see in this picture, the brilliant mountains in the background are swathed in rain clouds. And large ditches carry the necessary water into the fields. Nearly six million dollars was spent on the irrigation system for one plantation alone, and there are twenty-seven plantations scattered throughout the Islands. The men needed to work in the cane fields had to be imported from many countries during the past hundred years. That is the reason for Hawaii's diverse population. The owners of the sugar plantations were white settlers, called Haoles (HOW-*lays*) by the islanders. When they discovered that the growing, milling and transporting of sugar were large-scale operations, they banded together, and plantations, mills and a shipping company eventually came under the domination of a small group. This group of sugar factors or agencies is known as the Big Five, and it controls and directs a large part of the Hawaiian economy, although, since the war, mainland firms have moved in.

The men in the cane field here are working under the watchful eye of a *luna*, or overseer. Since World War II, their working conditions have changed considerably and they are unionized. Now they are the highest-paid sugar workers in the world.

SILVERSWORD PLANT: VOLCANIC RARITY

HALEAKALA is part of Hawaii National Park, and there is an excellent road leading to its rim. We can take a horseback trip across the desolate crater floor, and may even arrange to spend the night in a cabin there. This is surely one of the most unique experiences to be found on the face of the earth, and we have the eerie sensation that we have moved to another planet, for there is nothing here that seems to be familiar or even related to life as we know it. Now it is a moonscape that we see, with dead cinder cones rising from the crater floor, all in muted colors of black, lavender, orange and red. Odd plants are spotted among the volcanic rock, giving the whole scene an other-world unreality.

The unusual spiked ball in this picture is one of the rarest sights in the world. It is the silversword plant which grows only in the crater of Haleakala, the world's largest dormant volcano, which is in the eastern part of Maui. The plant actually resembles something you might expect to find at the bottom of the sea instead of 10,000 feet above sea level—its swords radiate from a central core, and they have a silvery aluminum color that contrasts strangely with the burnt cindery lava from which they grow. Once in its lifetime the silversword blossoms. Then it sends up a central shaft abloom with reddish-brown flowers. Seeds for new silverswords come from those blossoms, and the old silversword withers and dies.

The crater of an active volcano is like a giant bowl, holding a lake of molten lava.

ISLE OF KAUAI: PACIFIC LIGHTHOUSE

KAUAI is the oldest and the fourth largest of the islands, lying at the western end of the chain. Its windward shore points north into the Pacific, which stretches for endless blue miles toward the horizon. On this spur of land near Kalihiwai (*kah-lih-hih*-VY) Bay stands a lighthouse said to be the largest of its kind in the world. It looks lonely and inaccessible in this picture, but actually the entire island of Kauai is only twenty-five miles across, and there are excellent roads on it, built for the transport of sugar.

This little Garden Isle encompasses an amazing variety of scenic landscapes in its small area. It is all just one very large and ancient volcano, with a margin of lowlands on its south and east shores. The cones and craters have worn away over the centuries, and the raw rock is covered now with lush and verdant growth.

History was made on Kauai. There are traces of the earliest inhabitants of Hawaii found here, and legends and folklore enrich nearly every place on the island. It was on one of Kauai's beaches that Captain Cook first landed and was welcomed as a god. And on a bluff above the captain's beach, the Russians tried to gain a foothold in Hawaii in the early nineteenth century. The ruins of their fort, now crumbling and overgrown with weeds, are a memento of their ill-fated attempt to capture the island. At that time it was independent of the rest of Hawaii, which was ruled by powerful Kamehameha.

Kauai was the cradle of the infant sugar industry. In 1835 the first sugar mill in Hawaii was erected here. Two years later the first commercial sugar—two tons of it—was produced on this island. The old sugar mill is still standing, though in ruins, and it seems remarkable that from this small beginning a giant industry sprang.

NET MENDER: AGE-OLD SKILL

ON ALL the Hawaiian Islands fishing is a serious sport. The Polynesian ancestors of these people were traditionally great fishermen, and the modern Hawaiians have not lost their skill. This old fellow's hands may be gnarled, but they are knowing; and he handles a net with the ease born of long practice.

One of the islanders' most entertaining treats is a *hukilau* (*hoo-key*-LAU), which is something like a good old-fashioned fish fry. An enormous net is towed out a little distance from the shore. The people form into a long line in the shallow water, and they grab hold of ropes attached to the net. Then slowly and all together they haul it in to shore. There is great suspense and a good deal of joking during the haul, since no one will know until the net has been pulled in if there are enough fish in it to feed the several hundred people attending the *hukilau*. In case the fish are in short supply, there is often a pig roasting in an imu for emergency rations.

A very famous *hukilau* is held in a little village called Kalihiwai. The tidal wave of 1946, which did such terrible damage to Hilo, completely washed out Kalihiwai. Now the village has been rebuilt, and people from all over Kauai come to its beach at the edge of a deep blue bay for a real native *hukilau* that is one of the Islands' treats.

The hukilau is a fishy festival, and this net haul guarantees everyone a good feast.

WAIMEA CANYON: NATURE'S MASTERPIECE

THE most remarkable visual treat on Kauai is this multi-colored canyon carved deep in the volcanic rock. For twenty-five square miles this wonderland spreads out in scenic splendor, its colors re-creating the fiery tones of past eruptions. It has, naturally, reminded visitors of the Grand Canyon, but Waimea seems even more breath-taking, for we see it on a small tropical island.

The Waimea River and its branches carved this kingdom of gorges and peaks. In some places the gorge is 3,000 feet deep. The water power that did all this digging and carving came from Mt. Waialeale (*wy*-AH-*lee*-AH-*lee*), a few miles to the east. This is one of the wettest spots on earth, with an average yearly rainfall of 480 inches. Waialeale, with its attraction for rain clouds, has been responsible for the lush greenery of the Garden Isle, for the sugar, pineapple and rice grown here and for the rivers—larger than most in Hawaii.

There is an excellent road that follows the canyon, and along the way the Waimea Lookout is the place to stop. In the morning the canyon is colored soft blue and green with subtle shiftings from shade to shade. Later in the day the walls of the gorges take on coppery tints, and patches of brilliant red play in and out of the green. Clouds dapple the carved landscape, and the colors change suddenly as bright sunshine alternates with misty clouds sweeping over the vast canyon.

The inescapable hula girl is here at the canyon's edge. She makes a refreshingly different guide, and her sight-seeing lectures are uniquely dramatized with hula talk.

WAILUA RIVER: HAVEN OF TRANQUILLITY

WE HAVE traveled across to the eastern coast of Kauai now, and are in a region steeped in the legends and history of old Hawaii. Here the Wailua (*wy*-LOO-*ah*) River winds picturesquely between banks ablaze with blossoming trees. A boat trip up the river takes passengers to the mysterious Fern Grotto, a vaulted cavern hung with dripping fronds. In this picture we are on a narrow lagoon near the river's mouth. The largest and oldest coconut grove in the Islands grows on the banks of this lagoon, and at one time it was the royal grove of Kauai. The island's last queen is buried on a hill overlooking it, and each year a pageant called "The Queen Returns" revives for a single evening the pagan ritual of her court.

Now, a resort hotel invites its guests to enjoy the peace and beauty of this royal Polynesian setting. In observation of the wise old Hawaiian Law of Replacement, new palm trees are planted every few years to replace the aging ones. Since palm trees live only for a hundred years or so, this must be done to keep the grove everlastingly young and flourishing.

As you can see, there are places of uncrowded charm and authentic interest in the Outer Islands. Waikiki Beach is not the only worthwhile place to stay in Hawaii. Motion picture companies have chosen this section of Kauai as the location for films like "South Pacific," because nowhere else has nature provided such a breathtaking backdrop.

People are dwarfed in the fern-hung grotto of Kauai where feasts of thanksgiving once were held.

RITUAL AT SUNDOWN: ANCIENT PAGEANTRY

HERE near the same lagoon, with the royal grove of coconut palms in the background, a colorful ceremony takes place each day at sunset. As the blue of the lagoon deepens to evening sapphire and the shadows lengthen in the palm grove, a figure out of old Hawaii appears on the lawn. He is a pure-blooded Hawaiian, and he is dressed in the ancestral malo (MAH-*low*), or loincloth, with a feathered cape and helmet. (This is not one of the examples of ancient featherwork—they are all museum pieces now, and of a much finer, more delicate texture than the modern ones used in pageants.)

The young man kneels on the lawn and blows some haunting notes—one of the traditional Hawaiian calls—on a conch horn. The four points of the compass are appealed to, as the sun drops lower. Then the young man picks up a lighted torch and runs with it to the palm grove, by now quite deep in shadows. Swinging his flaming torch, he sprints in and out among the trees, lighting the standards set in the ground. And another evening of tropical magic envelops the island.

One community of the very few pure-blooded Hawaiians left on the Islands clusters on a tiny island that trails off Kauai's lee shore like a dinghy. This is the privately owned island of Niihau (*nee-eh*-HAH-*oo*). In the 1850's the King of Hawaii sold the island to a Scottish widow, and her descendants own it today. The two hundred or so natives who live and work on the island are an isolated group, a little pocket of the old Hawaii. Though they are taught English in school, their language is really Hawaiian, spoken as their ancestors spoke it, unchanged by foreign influences.

HANALEI VALLEY: LAND OF BOUNTY

WE ARE looking at the verdant checkerboard of Hanalei (*hah-nah-*LAY-*ee*) Valley, one of the most fertile of the entire Garden Isle. In the background Mt. Waialeale, the great rain-catcher, appears with its ranks of clouds lining up near the summit even on this day of brilliant sunshine. Hawaiian legend calls this valley "The Birthplace of Rainbows," and it is possible that the constant interplay of rain and sunshine gives the folk tale some basis of truth.

Two important Hawaiian foods grow in this valley—taro, a potato-like plant from which poi is made, and rice. Rice was farmed to a large extent by immigrant Chinese and Japanese, who left their backbreaking jobs on the sugar and pineapple plantations to work for themselves. Laboring in rice paddies was equally hard, but at least it was more familiar to Orientals. When the grain is ripening, you may see one of the time-honored Oriental contrivances in the fields. A web of crisscrossing strings is set up over the rice and hung with empty cans. An old woman of the family sits patiently at the edge of the paddy twitching the web and causing the cans to jangle and ring. This keeps any thieving birds from feasting on the rice grains that are ripening. It also fills the valley with a curious dissonant music, strange and romantic to any listener but the birds.

The thrilling story of Hawaii's discovery is told and retold in ancient chants.

POI DANCE: FOOD CELEBRATION

AT THE foot of Hanalei Valley, near the town of the same name, an old Hawaiian temple stands on a rise of ground. It was sacred to the goddess of the hula, whose early home was in Hanalei. In this picture we see one of the many variations of the dance, in which the pounding of poi from taro root is being dramatized. There were hundreds of different hulas, and through them the old traditions and culture were handed down. The man pounding poi with a heavy pestle in the hollowed wooden mortar is using implements that remain essentially unchanged from the earliest times on the Islands.

When the first Polynesians sailed to Hawaii, they brought certain native foods with them, including taro. This they planted in raised beds which were ingeniously irrigated. The starchy root of the taro was pounded into a thick paste called poi, and this, plus the fish caught in nearby waters, was their principal food. During all the centuries from their arrival on the Islands to Captain Cook's epochal discovery, the Hawaiians' ways remained the same. Now, however, poi is made commercially, and it is usually only in the hula that the traditional pounding is performed as it used to be.

When King Kalakaua decided to have a spectacular coronation ceremony for himself in 1883, among its features were performances of 262 different kinds of hula. This poi dance might well have been one of them. A famous guest at the coronation, Robert Louis Stevenson, found the island dances far less exciting than other tourists have. He derided the hula with the comment: "Surely the most dull of man's inventions, and the spectator yawns under its length as at a college lecture or a parliamentary debate." Well, that was nearly eighty years ago, and Stevenson's judgment must have been a minority one.

PINEAPPLE FIELDS: THE FRUITFUL EARTH

THIS is a pineapple field on Kauai Island, where the red earth lends color to the landscape and makes a bright contrast to the leafy plants. The sharp cliffs rising in the background add a touch of grandeur to this big business operation. The pineapple industry is Hawaii's second largest, and she supplies 55 per cent of the world market for the fresh fruit.

Because pineapples must become fully ripe on the plant and they deteriorate when shipped long distances, most Hawaiian pineapples are canned for export. The canneries on Oahu are enormous, and their machinery is almost human. One series of operations peels, cores and slices the fruit to just the size for canning. It is graded and packed by women on the assembly lines, then sealed, steam-cooked and labeled—all in an incredible quarter of an hour.

Nature's share in the operation takes a good deal longer. Fifteen to twenty months after the first planting, the pineapple flowers, and the fruit ripens five or six months after that. As we look over this neatly planted field, it is hard to imagine the enormous amount of work that went into it. Roads, such as the one we are on now, are planned at hundred-foot intervals for sprayers and long-armed harvesters. Then machines travel over the fields, laying down long strips of specially treated mulch paper. The pineapple slips are planted through holes in the paper, and moisture and heat are held in the ground, while weeds are discouraged. This remarkable paper is a Hawaiian invention.

If we could pick a ripe pineapple out of the field now and eat it, the taste would be surprisingly delicious. Hawaiian pineapple is superior to the fruit from Mexico, Cuba and Puerto Rico, but unfortunately Hawaii is too far away from most markets to make shipping the fresh fruit practical.

LIVING LEGEND: HAWAII'S PROUD PAST

NOW we have returned to the black volcanic beach on the Big Island. Facing eastward across the Pacific to the Americas stands the figure of Kamehameha the Great, living again in a commemorative pageant. This descendant of old Hawaii is wrapped in a modern version of the fabulous golden cape of royal feathers and crowned with a matching helmet. The original yellow cloak of Kamehameha is supposed to have been over a hundred years in the making. To create a cloak like that, at least ten thousand birds had to be stripped of their plumage. Now the island feather birds are very rare, if not extinct, and the art is a lost one. Hawaii is no longer a kingdom, and Kamehameha's people have dwindled. But the best of their traditions and culture exists today, woven into the fabric of the life of the islands.

A daughter of a Hawaiian mother and Caucasian father expressed it this way, speaking to an American writer: "My mother's people would look at the sunrise and say how beautiful it is. They would sit and fish and look at the sun and enjoy it. My father's people would look at the sun and ask: 'How far is it and how much does it weigh?' " In twentieth-century Hawaii, love of natural beauty is happily linked with technological advances.

Skimming the crests of breakers off Diamond Head, these young Hawaiians are still masters of the elements.

SOME IMPORTANT DATES IN HAWAIIAN HISTORY

500 A.D.	*First Polynesians reach Hawaii from Samoa or Tahiti.*
1778	*English navigator, Capt. James Cook, lands at Waimea on the island of Kauai. First white man to discover the Hawaiian Islands.*
1779	*Cook is killed by natives.*
1782	*King Kamehameha I ascends throne of one of four kingdoms of Hawaii; conquers all the islands except Kauai; consolidates the kingdom in 1810.*
1819	*On death of King Kamehameha I, old religion and taboo system are abolished.*
1820	*First American missionaries, led by Bingham family, come to Hawaii from Boston.*
1823	*Queen Keopuolani first Christian convert.*
1854	*Negotiations are opened for annexation of Hawaii to the United States. First negotiations unsuccessful.*
1876	*Reciprocity treaty with United States. One year later U.S. is given exclusive right to use Pearl Harbor.*
1893	*Last of the Hawaiian rulers, Queen Liliuokalani, is deposed. Provisional government is established.*
1894	*Republic of Hawaii is established on July 4.*
1898	*Annexation of Hawaii is accepted by a joint resolution of Congress.*
1900	*Hawaii becomes a territory of the United States.*
1941	*Japanese bomb Pearl Harbor, December 7; United States enters the Second World War; Hawaii is placed under martial law.*
1944	*Martial law is repealed by President Franklin D. Roosevelt; danger of invasion of the islands has passed.*
1950	*Hawaii prepares state constitution, ratified by a general election, to implement drive for statehood.*
1959	*U.S. Congress approves Hawaiian statehood on March 12.*
1959	*Hawaii officially becomes the 50th State, August 21.*

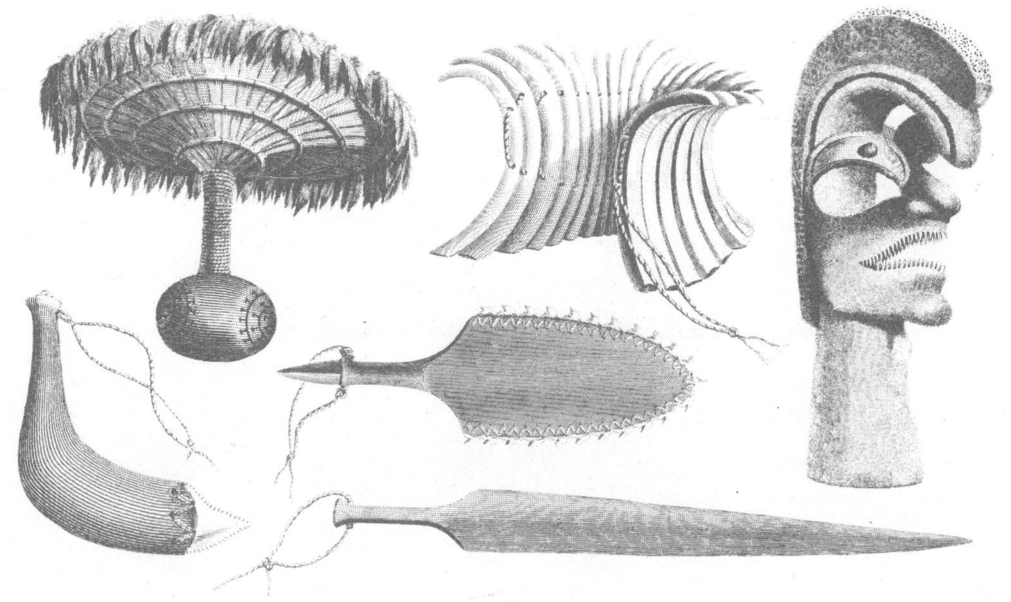

SOME FAMOUS NAMES IN HAWAIIAN HISTORY

CAPTAIN JAMES COOK (1728-1779)—*English naval captain, discovered the Hawaiian Islands January 1778, named them the Sandwich Islands. Killed in a native uprising on the island of Hawaii in 1779.*

KING KAMEHAMEHA I (1736-1819) — *Hawaii's greatest king. United the islands, consolidating the kingdom in 1810. His dynasty followed his strong rule, changing Hawaii from a primitive pagan culture to a modern Christian kingdom.*

HIRAM BINGHAM (1789-1869)—*American missionary, came to Hawaii from Boston. Founder of the Punahou Academy.*

KAMEHAMEHA II (ruled 1819-1824)—*Called Liholiho. Visited England in 1823 with his wife. They died there of the measles.*

KAPIOLANI—*In 1824 this wife of a chief defied Pele, the volcano goddess, and prayed to the Christian God instead.*

KAMEHAMEHA III (ruled 1825-1854)—*Had queen of Kamehameha I as his regent, and this began practice of having a regent, usually female, in every reign. Written constitution, parliament, taxes and criminal code established. Great Mahele, or division of land, took place.*

KAMEHAMEHA IV (ruled 1854-1863)—*Golden Age of Hawaiian royalty. He and his queen visited England. Queen Emma and Queen Victoria became friends.*

DAVID KALAKAUA (ruled 1874-1891)—*Playboy king who won election to throne against Anglophile Queen Emma. Signed treaty with United States in 1876. Had fabulous coronation in 1883. Main shopping street in Waikiki is named for him.*

QUEEN LILIUOKALANI (1838-1917)—*The last of Hawaii's rulers. Wrote "Aloha Oe." Deposed so that provisional government could be set up with the intention of achieving annexation to the United States.*

SANFORD B. DOLE (1844-1926)—*Hawaiian son of American missionaries. Became President of the Republic of Hawaii in 1894. Appointed first territorial governor in 1900 when Hawaii was annexed.*

GOVERNOR WILLIAM F. QUINN (1919-)—*The first governor of the new state of Hawaii. Born in Rochester, New York.*

SENATOR HIRAM L. FONG (1907-)—*One of the first two Senators from Hawaii, the first Oriental to serve in the Senate.*

SENATOR OREN E. LONG (1889-)—*Hawaii's other first member of the United States Senate.*

DANIEL K. INOUYE (1925–)—*Hawaii's first Congressman, now a Senator.*

SOME HAWAIIAN WORDS AND PHRASES

Here is a list of words and phrases that you might be likely to use when traveling in Hawaii. The words are written in simple phonetics for the Hawaiian pronunciation, with the accented syllable in capitals.

Hello, farewell	Aloha *(ah-LOW-hah)*
Foreign visitor, tourist	Haole *(HOW-lay)*
Newcomer (resident)	Malihini *(mah-lih-HEE-nee)*
Old-time resident	Kamaaina *(kah-mah-EYE-nah)*
Friend	Aikane *(eye-KAH-nee)*
Man	Kane *(KAH-nee)*
Woman	Wahine *(wah-HEE-nee)*
Child	Keiki *(KAY-kee)*
Beach or Seashore	Kahakai *(KAH-hah-kah-ee)*
Cliff	Pali *(PAH-lee)*
Mountain	Mauna *(MAW-nah)*
Street	Alanui *(ah-lah-NOO-ee)*
Where is . . . ?	Mahea *(mah-HAY-ah)*
Hotel	Hokele *(hoh-KAY-lay)*
Airplane	Mokulele *(moh-koo-LAY-lay)*
Taxi	Kaa hoolimalima *(kah-ah hoh-OH-lee-mah-lee-mah)*
Train	Kaahi *(kah-AH-hee)*
Ship	Moku *(MOH-koo)*
Harbor	Awa *(AH-wah)*
Restaurant	Hale aina *(HAH-lay EYE-nah)*
Directions: To the sea	Makai *(mah-KAH-ee)*
To the mountains	Mauka *(MAU-kah)*
Come here	Hele mai *(HAY-lay mah-ee)*
Thank you	Mahalo *(mah-HAH-low)*

DAYS OF THE WEEK

Sunday	La Pule *(lah POO-lay)*	Today	Keia la *(kay-EE-ah lah)*
Monday	Poakahi *(poh-ah-KAH-hee)*	Tomorrow	Apopo *(ah-poh-POH)*
Tuesday	Poalua *(poh-ah-LOO-ah)*	Yesterday	Inehinei *(ee-NAY-hee-nay-ee)*
Wednesday	Poakolu *(poh-ah-KOH-loo)*	Tonight	Keia po *(kay-EE-ah poh)*
Thursday	Poaha *(poh-ah-HAH)*	Week	Pule *(POO-lay)*
Friday	Poalima *(poh-ah-LEE-mah)*	Month	Malama *(mah-LAH-mah)*
Saturday	Poaono *(poh-ah-OH-noh)*	Year	Makahiki *(mah-kah-HEE-kee)*

NUMBERS

One	Kahi *(KAH-hee)*
Two	Lua *(LOO-ah)*
Three	Kolu *(KOH-loo)*
Four	Ha *(hah)*
Five	Lima *(LEE-mah)*
Six	Ono *(OH-noo)*
Seven	Hiku *(HEE-koo)*
Eight	Walu *(WAH-loo)*
Nine	Iwa *(EE-wah)*
Ten	Umi *(OO-mee)*
One hundred	Haneli *(hah-NAY-lee)*
One thousand	Kaukani *(kah-oo-KAH-nee)*

FOODS

Food	Kaukau *(kow-kow)*
Breakfast	Aina kakahiaka *(EYE-nah kah-kah-HEE-ah-kah)*
Lunch	Aina awakea *(EYE-nah ahv-ah-KAY-ah)*
Dinner	Aina nui *(EYE-nah NOO-ee)*
Fish	Ia *(EE-ah)*
Pig	Pua'a *(POO-ah-ah)*
Chicken	Moa *(MOH-ah)*
Coffee	Kope *(KOH-pay)*

INDEX